Quick Quin

by David Nguyen
illustrated by Olivia Cole

Core Decodable 57

Bothell, WA • Chicago, IL • Columbus, OH • New York, NY

MHEonline.com

Copyright © 2015 McGraw-Hill Education

All rights reserved. No part of this publication may be reproduced or distributed in any form or by any means, or stored in a database or retrieval system, without the prior written consent of McGraw-Hill Education, including, but not limited to, network storage or transmission, or broadcast for distance learning.

Send all inquiries to:
McGraw-Hill Education
8787 Orion Place
Columbus, OH 43240

ISBN: 978-0-02-136202-8
MHID: 0-02-136202-5

Printed in the United States of America.

2 3 4 5 6 7 8 9 DOC 20 19 18 17 16 15

Quin sat on her porch.
She rested on a quilt.

Quin was hot on her porch.
She squirted lemon in her drink.

Max was squirming on Quin.
"Quit squirming, Max," she said.

Max did not quit squirming.
He hit her drink.

Quin was quick.
She got her glass.

Did the liquid get on the quilt?
Not a drop got on the quilt!